HERA

QUEEN OF THE GREEK GODS

by Tammy Gagne

Content Consultant
Susan C. Shelmerdine, PhD,
Professor of Classical Studies
University of North Carolina, Greensboro
Greensboro, NC

CAPSTONE PRESS
a capstone imprint

Snap Books are published by Capstone Press,
1710 Roe Crest Drive, North Mankato, Minnesota 56003
www.mycapstone.com

Library of Congress Cataloging-in-Publication Data
Names: Gagne, Tammy, author.
Title: Hera : queen of the Greek gods / by Tammy Gagne.
Description: North Mankato: Capstone Press, 2019. | Series: Snap Books.
  Legendary goddesses | Includes index.
Identifiers: LCCN 2018036725| ISBN 9781543554533 (library binding) |
ISBN 9781543559163 (pbk.) | ISBN 9781543554571 (ebook pdf)
Subjects: LCSH: Hera (Greek deity)—Juvenile literature.
Classification: LCC BL820.J6 G34 2018. | DDC 292.2/114—dc23
LC record available at https://lccn.loc.gov/2018036725

Editorial Credits
Gina Kammer, editor
Bobbie Nuytten, designer
Svetlana Zhurkin, media researcher
Katy LaVigne, production specialist

Image Credits
Alamy: AF Fotografie, 5 (left), Interfoto, 23 (top); Bridgeman Images: The
Stapleton Collection/Private Collection/Semele is Deceived or Semele
Ingannata da Giunone, illustration from Ovid's Metamorphoses, Florence,
1832 (hand-colored engraving), Ademollo, Luigi (1764-1849), 19; Dreamstime:
Iryna Momot, 7 (top); Getty Images: De Agostini Picture Library, 9, DEA
Picture Library, 13, DEA/G. Dagli Orti, 5 (right), 16; iStockphoto: benoitb,
18, duncan1890, 12, 26, Nastasic, 10, 11 (right), ZU_09, 7 (bottom), 8, 23
(bottom right); Newscom: Album/Fine Art Images, 20, Album/Prisma, 25,
Heritage Images/CM Dixon, 11 (left), Universal Images Group/Leemage, 17;
Shutterstock: Digital Storm, 23 (middle), Dlinnychulok, 4, Elena Shchipkova,
6, Eric Isselee, 22, itechno, 21, Luxerendering, 27 (left), Masterrr, 14, 15,
MatiasDelCarmine, 29, Mikhail Yuryev, 24, RAndrei, 28 (left), Sergey
Goryachev, cover, WitR, 28 (right); The Metropolitan Museum of Art, Public
Domain, 23 (bottom left); Wikimedia: Canino Collection, 27 (right)

Design Elements by Shutterstock

Printed and bound in the USA.
PA49

TABLE OF CONTENTS

Chapter 1

QUEEN OF THE GREEK GODS

Hera was the Greek goddess of marriage. One of the main myths about Hera tells how she also became the queen of the gods. In ancient Greece, the supreme god Zeus fell in love with the goddess Hera before she returned his feelings. But he wasn't sure how to approach her. To get Hera's attention, Zeus created a powerful storm and turned himself into a small bird called a cuckoo. Many gods and goddesses could change themselves into animals and other things when they wanted. As the bird, Zeus perched on the ledge outside Hera's window.

Upon seeing the tiny creature alone in the harsh weather, Hera rushed to its rescue. She invited the bird inside to get warm and dry. Finally, he had won her over. Zeus could not wait another minute. He transformed himself back into his own image. He quickly asked the goddess to become his wife. She agreed.

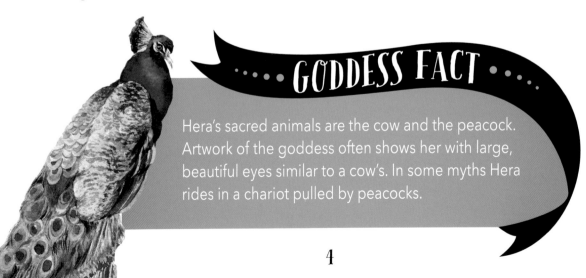

GODDESS FACT

Hera's sacred animals are the cow and the peacock. Artwork of the goddess often shows her with large, beautiful eyes similar to a cow's. In some myths Hera rides in a chariot pulled by peacocks.

Their wedding took place in the Garden of Hesperides. It was a simple yet sacred event. Hera wore a beautiful gown. After the ceremony, she took her place on a golden throne beside her new husband. As the wife of the king of all gods, Hera became their queen.

Each wedding guest brought a gift for the happy couple. But one gift stood out among all the others. Gaia, the earth goddess, gave Hera a tree that produced golden apples. Hera planted the tree in her garden.

Three nymphs called the Hesperides guarded the tree with the golden apples.

THE STORIES OF GREEK MYTHOLOGY

Myths like the story about Zeus and Hera's wedding were an important part of everyday life for the ancient Greeks. They looked to myths for answers about how the world came to be. These stories also helped people explain complex events such as the weather and natural disasters. The ancient Greeks believed that gods and goddesses controlled the world from the top of Mount Olympus.

Zeus and Hera played large parts in many Greek myths. While they loved each other deeply, their behavior did not always show it. Much like human beings, the Greek gods and goddesses were far from perfect. They often felt intense jealousy and anger. And they sometimes fought and lied. But none of these things stopped the ancient Greeks from admiring their Olympic **Pantheon**. The religion of the ancient Greeks was based on worshipping Zeus, Hera, and the other Greek gods and goddesses.

Mount Olympus rises over the Greek landscape. It is the highest mountain in Greece at 9,570 feet (2,917 meters).

The Goddess of Marriage, Family, and Childbirth

In addition to being the queen of the all the gods, Hera also became the goddess of marriage, family, and childbirth. The ancient Greeks built temples to honor her. Women would visit these **temples** to pray to the goddess.

Wives believed that Hera would help them make their own marriages successful. Some women would call on her when they wanted to become mothers. Women already expecting babies would pray to her for help in delivering healthy infants.

a Greek wedding

pantheon—all the gods of a particular mythology
temple—a building used for worship

Chapter 2

THE CREATION OF HERA

Hera's parents were Titans. These were the first gods created by Gaia and Uranus—the gods of the earth and the sky. Hera's father was Cronus, the King of the Titans. Her mother was Rhea. The Titans were known for having few limits. They did and said whatever they wished. And they didn't care about how their actions affected anyone else.

Gaia and Uranus could see into the future. They warned Cronus that one of his children would one day take his throne away from him. But Cronus believed that he could keep this from happening. Each time Rhea gave birth, Cronus swallowed the child immediately. He did this when Hera was born too.

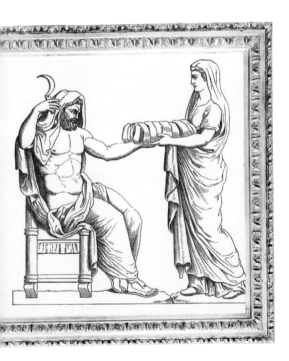

Rhea tricks Cronus with a stone wrapped in a blanket.

After the fifth birth, however, Rhea hatched a plan. To save her sixth child, Rhea decided to trick Cronus by wrapping a stone in the infant's blanket. Cronus swallowed the stone so quickly that he did not even realize that it wasn't the child. This made it possible for the last child, Zeus, to survive. Rhea hid Zeus away until he was old enough to fight his father for the throne. When he was ready, Zeus came to his father and forced him to spit out his swallowed children—Zeus' siblings. Zeus saved the lives of Hestia, Hera, Demeter, Hades, and Poseidon.

GODDESS FACT

Cronus spit out his children in the reverse order of their birth. Hestia, born first, was spit out last.

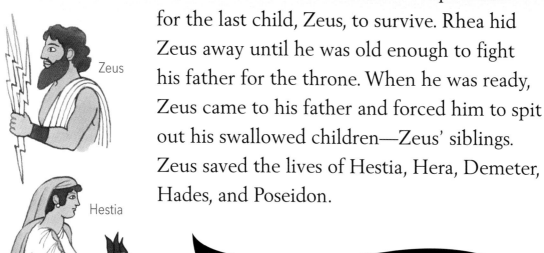

Zeus

Hestia

Hera

Demeter

Hades

Poseidon

TAKING OVER MOUNT OLYMPUS

With the help of his brothers and sisters, Zeus took the throne from Cronus. They also began the fight to remove the rest of the Titans from Mount Olympus. But the Titans would not go down without a fight. The War of the Titans was long and brutal. But eventually Zeus, Hera, and their siblings won.

The siblings then took over the roles the Titans had served. In addition to leading the other gods, Zeus became the ruler of the sky. Hades became the god of the dead, while Poseidon took the job of ruling the sea. Demeter became goddess of the harvest while Hestia ruled home and **hearth**. Hera, like Zeus, had more than one role. Although she became the goddess of marriage and family, she also became the queen of the gods.

hearth—home, also the area in front of a fireplace

The gods battle the Titans and win.

GODDESS FACT

When the war was over, the new Olympian gods sent the Titans to the Tartaros. This was a pit below the ancient Greek underworld, the realm of Hades.

Wife or Sister? Both!

Some people wonder how Hera can be both the wife of Zeus and his own sister. It actually was not unusual for Greek gods and goddesses to marry their siblings. There was no moral judgment about this practice.

Many of the Titans had also married their siblings. Like Zeus and Hera, Cronus and Rhea were also brother and sister.

the marriage of Hera and Zeus

Zeus and Hera ruling from Olympus

Chapter 3

HERA AND HER FAMILY

Zeus and Hera began their reign as the leaders of the new Olympic pantheon. They also had three children of their own. Their son Ares became the god of war. Hebe became the goddess of youth. A second daughter, Eileithyia, became the goddess of childbirth. But when Zeus gave birth to the goddess Athena all on his own, Hera was furious. She responded by creating Hephaistos, a child that was just her own. But she was devastated when she saw that he was **deformed**. She was so disappointed that she threw him off Mount Olympus, injuring him greatly in both body and spirit. After returning to Mount Olympus, Hephaistos later sided with his mother when she and Zeus were arguing. In anger Zeus flung him from Olympus once again. He landed, wounded, on the island of Lemnos and lived with the people there.

Hebe, the goddess of youth

Hera's marriage to Zeus was a rocky one. Zeus did not always stay true to his wife. He had children with other goddesses, **nymphs**, and human women. Hera became intensely jealous and angry. But because Zeus was the leader of the gods, Hera could not take her anger out on him. Instead, she got revenge on the other females and their children.

deformed—twisted, bent, or disfigured

nymph—a minor female goddess who lives on earth

·····• GODDESS FACT •·····

Hera often got revenge on her husband's love interests in creative ways. When Zeus fell in love with Callisto, Hera transformed the nymph into a bear. To keep her safe from hunters, Zeus later turned Callisto into the constellation The Big Bear, which contains the Big Dipper.

Hera's Family Tree

The queen of the gods and goddess of marriage was both the wife and sister of Zeus. Hera had five siblings. With Zeus, Hera had three children: Ares, Hebe, and Eileithyia. Because Zeus had his daughter Athena on his own, Hera had her son Hephaistos on her own.

RHEA

Hera's mother was a Titan, one of the children of Gaia and Uranus.

Gaia

Uranus

HERA

The king of the Titans swallowed his daughter just after she was born.

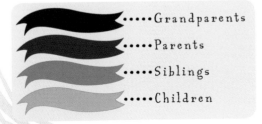

CRONUS

····· Grandparents

····· Parents

····· Siblings

····· Children

14

The god of the dead and the underworld was Hera's brother.

HADES

goddess of wisdom and war

ATHENA

The goddess of agriculture was Hera's sister.

DEMETER

goddess of youth

HEBE

Hera had three children with her husband. Zeus had Athena on his own.

ZEUS

god of war

ARES

Hera's sister Hestia was the goddess of the home and hearth.

HESTIA

goddess of childbirth

EILEITHYIA

Hera's brother Poseidon was the god of the sea.

POSEIDON

god of fire

HEPHAISTOS

A LESSON NOT LEARNED

Hera's greatest effort at revenge came when Zeus fell in love with a human named Alcmene. When Hera learned that Alcmene was carrying Zeus' child, she asked for Eileithyia's help. She hoped that her daughter could use her powers to stop the birth. But that plan did not work. Alcmene delivered a son named Heracles. But Hera was not done yet. She tried to kill the child by placing two enormous snakes in his cradle. The snakes were no match for the powerful infant. He crushed them with his bare hands.

Zeus could not deal with Hera's jealousy any longer. He decided it was time to teach his vengeful wife a lesson. Zeus hung her by her wrists from the top of Mount Olympus. And to make things even more uncomfortable, he placed heavy **anvils** on her feet. Hera's cries could be heard throughout the sky. But no one dared to help her for fear of Zeus. He agreed to let her go the next morning if she stopped trying to get revenge. She agreed, but her promise was an empty one. She kept seeking revenge on her husband through those he had relationships with and their children.

anvil—a heavy iron block with a flat top

Only a child, Heracles kills the snakes Hera sent to kill him.

GODDESS FACT

Although Zeus had many other romantic relationships, Hera, as the goddess of marriage, always remained true to him.

Hera's Golden Throne

Hera passed on her talent for revenge to Hephaistos, but he used it against her. As the god of fire and metal work, he built his mother a beautiful throne made of gold. But when she sat in the chair, she realized that invisible chains kept her from leaving it.

Dionysus, the god of wine, stepped in to help Hera. After drinking too much wine with Dionysus, Hephaistos finally agreed to free his mother in exchange for being allowed back up onto Mount Olympus.

17

Chapter 4

HERA'S POWERS AND WEAKNESSES

Hera had many special powers. Like all the Olympic gods and goddesses, she was **immortal**. She could also transform herself and others into different beings. She had absolute power over her areas of marriage, family, and childbirth.

Hera also had great speed and strength. She supported the Greeks in the Trojan War. Artemis, the goddess of hunting, supported the people of Troy. When Artemis challenged Hera on the battlefield, the **archer** was confident. But the queen quickly snatched Artemis' bow and arrows. They were gone before Artemis even knew what had happened.

Artemis

GODDESS FACT

Artemis is the daughter of Zeus and the Titan Leto. Artemis' twin brother Apollo is the god of the sun.

Hera's greatest weapon was her clever mind. When Zeus fell in love with a human named Semele, Hera disguised herself as the young woman's nurse. She encouraged Semele to ask Zeus to show her his true form. As a goddess, Hera had no trouble being in the presence of the god in all his glory. The storms and thunderbolts that came along with him never hurt her. But she knew they were too much for a mortal. Semele asked Zeus to grant

Disguised as her nurse, Hera tricks Semele.

her one wish. He had already promised it to her before she revealed what she wanted. Just as Hera had imagined, the god's shining form killed his human mistress. Without ever lifting a finger of her own, Hera had killed Semele.

immortal—someone who lives forever
archer—a person who shoots a bow and arrow

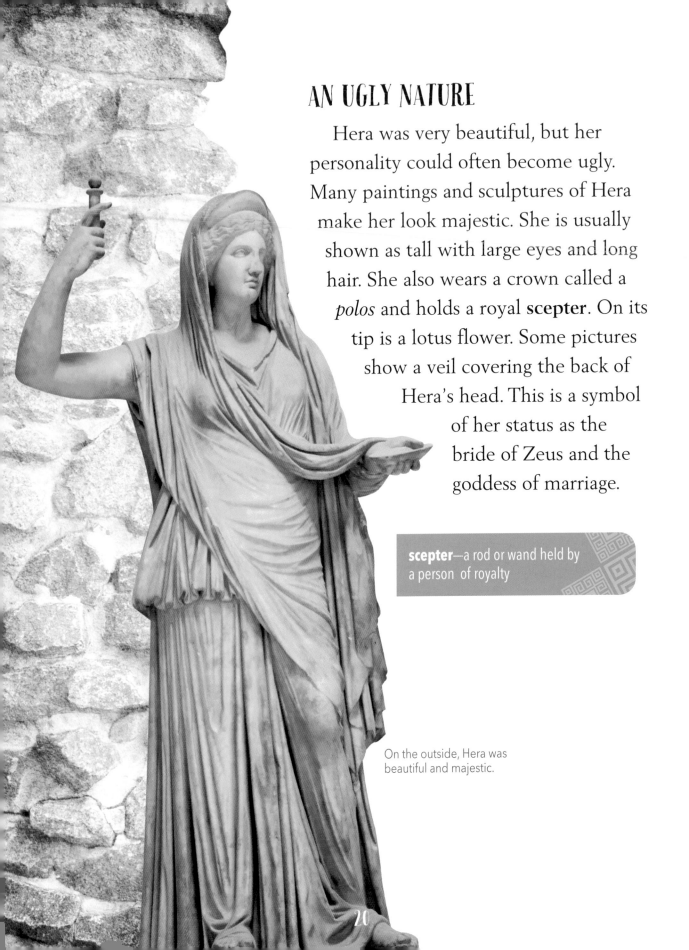

AN UGLY NATURE

Hera was very beautiful, but her personality could often become ugly. Many paintings and sculptures of Hera make her look majestic. She is usually shown as tall with large eyes and long hair. She also wears a crown called a *polos* and holds a royal **scepter**. On its tip is a lotus flower. Some pictures show a veil covering the back of Hera's head. This is a symbol of her status as the bride of Zeus and the goddess of marriage.

scepter—a rod or wand held by a person of royalty

On the outside, Hera was beautiful and majestic.

Many Greek myths describe Hera as the most beautiful Greek goddess—even more so than Aphrodite, the goddess of love. But a Trojan named Paris did not agree. When he named Aphrodite the winner of a beauty contest over the queen, Hera was determined to ruin him. Her support of the Greeks in the Trojan War was inspired by her hatred for Paris. Hera's constant desire for revenge led her to be known as much for her jealousy as for her role as the goddess of marriage. Although she was beautiful on the outside, Hera's vengeful personality made her less attractive.

GODDESS FACT

The ancient poet Homer was the first person to link Hera to the cow. In his epic poem the *Iliad*, Homer repeatedly calls the queen "cow-eyed Hera" because of her large, sweet eyes.

Hera and the Lion

Hera is most often linked to the cow and the peacock. But she is also associated with another animal—the lion. Some ancient Greek coins show Hera on one side and the head of a lion on the other. Other ancient statues of the goddess also include a lion at her side.

An ancient vase depicts Hera, Aphrodite, and Athena taking part in their contest for the golden apple. The vase shows Athena holding a helmet, one of her symbols. It also shows Aphrodite with Eros, whom she is often connected with. Hera holds a lion.

Hera trained the Nemean Lion. This lion had skin that couldn't be harmed by weapons. She set the lion in the hills of Nemea to attack the people living there until Heracles, a **demigod** son of Zeus, killed it with his bare hands. Hera then turned the lion into the constellation Leo.

demigod—someone who is part god and part human

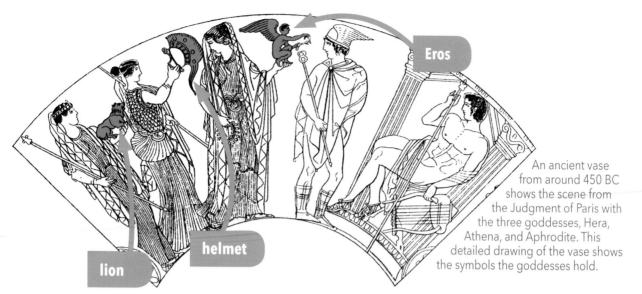

lion

helmet

Eros

An ancient vase from around 450 BC shows the scene from the Judgment of Paris with the three goddesses, Hera, Athena, and Aphrodite. This detailed drawing of the vase shows the symbols the goddesses hold.

Hera's Nemean Lion lives on as the constellation Leo. Connecting the cluster of stars makes the shape of a lion.

Hera sends out the Nemean Lion with the messenger Iris.

Heracles beat the Nemean Lion with his bare hands.

23

Chapter 5

HERA IN GREEK HISTORY AND MODERN CULTURE

Hera remains an important part of Greek history and culture. Her presence is still seen in the modern nation of Greece. A temple that honors the queen goddess stands in Olympia. Built around 600 BC, the Temple of Hera is one of the oldest temples in the country. It is even older than the temple that honors Zeus. Today both temples stand in ruins, much like other famous structures from the ancient era.

The ruins of the Temple of Hera still stand in Olympia, Greece.

The Temple of Hera has played a small part in the Olympic Games throughout history. The first games were held in Olympia in 776 BC. After the Temple of Hera was built, it became the location of many Olympic rituals. For example, the olive crowns the Greeks gave the victors were displayed on the Table of Kolotes inside the temple. The Greek Olympic Games came to an end by the year 400 AD. In 1896, nations around the world decided to hold them again. The Olympic torch relay tradition began in 1936. The torch-lighting **ritual** takes place in front of the Temple of Hera.

People travel from all over the world to visit the Greek ruins, including the Temple of Hera. Although time and war have damaged them greatly, these structures remain an important part of Greek culture. For some people, these structures are symbols of their heritage. Others regard them as pieces of world history.

ritual—a ceremony involving a set of actions that are always performed the same way

GODDESS FACT

A statue of Hera once stood in the temple named for the goddess. The stone queen sat on her throne with Zeus standing by her side. Today, no statue remains. However, the head of a statue was found near the building. It may be the goddess' head.

The Hera Festival

The ancient Greeks created the Olympic Games to honor Zeus. Only male athletes were allowed to take part in the contests at that time. A separate set of games existed to honor Hera. Unmarried girls were allowed to take part in games such as foot races.

Although the festival honored the goddess of marriage, it barred married women from taking part. Married women were also not allowed to watch the males compete in their games. The unmarried girls competing in their own races, however, were permitted to attend the men's games.

A contest during the ancient Olympic Games

SYMBOLS OF HERA

lotus flower

crown

royal scepter

HERA'S MODERN FOLLOWERS

Although most modern Greek citizens practice **Orthodox Christianity**, the ancient Greek religions play a part in many Greek festivals and other celebrations. A small number of people still practice the ancient religions. Called the Hellenes, they see the gods and goddesses as symbols of values such as beauty, health, and wisdom.

Samos, Greece

Argos, Greece

GODDESS FACT

Hera has long been linked to the Greek city Argos and the island Samos. Both Argos and Samos named her their **patron** during ancient times. Although she was worshipped throughout Greece, the ancient Greeks from these places considered her their own special goddess.

People still tell the stories about Hera and her fellow Olympic gods and goddesses throughout the modern world. Homer's epic poems the *Iliad* and the *Odyssey* are required reading for many high school and college literature courses. And many modern books and movies have been based on these and other tales from Greek mythology. The Percy Jackson books and film series even tell new stories about these characters.

No one knows for sure whether Hera, Zeus, and the other Greek gods ever existed as real people. The myths about them may seem too hard to believe for many readers. Others may find them old fashioned or outdated. But the Greeks once believed in their existence as gods, and their myths have lasted through time. The lessons these stories teach are as useful today as they were when they were first told in ancient Greece.

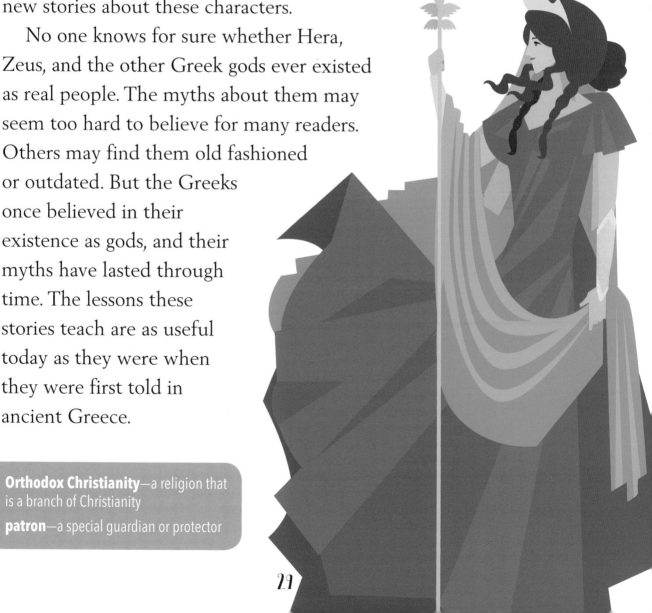

Orthodox Christianity—a religion that is a branch of Christianity

patron—a special guardian or protector

GLOSSARY

anvil (AN-vuhl)—a heavy iron block with a flat top

archer (AHR-chur)—a person who shoots with a bow and arrow

deformed (di-FORMD)—twisted, bent, or disfigured

demigod (DEM-ee-gahd)—someone who is part god and part human

hearth (HARTH)—a fireplace, a symbol of home

immortal (i-MOR-tuhl)—someone who lives forever

nymph (NIMF)—a minor female goddess who lives on earth

Orthodox Christianity (OR-thuh-doks kris-chee-AN-uh-tee)—a religion that is a branch of Christianity

pantheon (PAN-thee-on)—the gods of a particular mythology

patron (PAY-truhn)—a special guardian or protector

ritual (RICH-oo-uhl)—a ceremony involving a set of actions that are always performed in the same way

scepter (SEP-tuhr)—a rod or wand held by a person of royalty

temple (TEM-puhl)—a building used for worship

READ MORE

Hamilton, Edith. *Mythology: Timeless Tales of Gods and Heroes.* New York: Black Dog & Leventhal Publishers, 2017.

Loh-Hagan, Virginia. *Hera.* Gods and Goddesses of the Ancient World. Ann Arbor, Mich.: Cherry Lake Publishing, 2017.

Riordan, Rick. *Percy Jackson's Greek Gods.* Los Angeles: Disney-Hyperion, 2015.

Temple, Teri. *Hera.* Gods and Goddesses of Ancient Greece. New York: AV2 by Weigl, 2016.

INTERNET SITES

Use FactHound to find Internet sites related to this book.

Visit *www.facthound.com*

Just type in 9781543554533 and go!

Super-cool stuff! Check out projects, games and lots more at **www.capstonekids.com**

INDEX